Nurture Yourself First - Exercises to reduce stress and improve your life

Michelle Mckay

ISBN-13: 9781091094048

DEDICATION

To midwives , nurses, HCA's, paramedics and all within healthcare that
give so much of themselves to others

CONTENTS

"If you are kind, people may accuse you of selfish, ulterior motives: Be kind anyway. If you are successful you will win some false friends and true enemies: Succeed anyway. If you are honest and frank people will try to cheat you: Be honest anyway. What you spend years building, someone could destroy overnight: Build anyway. If you find serenity and happiness, they may be jealous of you: Be happy anyway. The good you do today, will often be forgotten by tomorrow: Do good anyway. Give the world the best you have, and it may never be enough: Give your best anyway." ~ Mother Teresa

"We ourselves feel that what we are doing is just a drop in the ocean. But the ocean would be less because of that missing drop." ~ Mother Teresa

1 INTRODUCTION

My mission in life is not merely to survive, but to thrive; and to do so with some passion, some compassion, some humor, and some style"

— Maya Angelou

Midwives and nurses provide support for the population under increasing pressures and funding cuts. This along with changes in legislation, training and workload has meant a reduction in retention rates and job satisfaction.

The introduction of reflection into healthcare aims to improve skills in identifying training needs, service development and self-care.

However, Midwives and nurses can sometimes feel that there is no way of coping with the demands of home and work commitments.

The aim of this journal is to introduce different self-help methods of coping with stress and a safe place to write down both positive and negative experiences.

In addition, at the end of each chapter is an activity to utilise each new method.

The journal can be used from start to finish or you can skip to the exercises that you feel are the most suitable for you at any given time.

Through the journal you will learn techniques such as mindfulness, hypnosis and guided relaxation, Neuro Linguistic Programming (NLP) and positive mindset affirmations.

Nurses, Midwives and other healthcare professionals give so much of themselves to others that I wanted to help in any small way to help them to care for themselves.

"No matter how many mistakes you make or how slow you progress, you are still way ahead of everyone who isn't trying." ~ Tony Robbins

2 HYPNOSIS

"If you say to yourself 'It's difficult to get up in the morning', 'It's hard to cease smoking', then you are already using hypnotic suggestions on yourself" ~ Richard Bandler

*"Hypnosis is a **trance** state characterized by **extreme suggestibility, relaxation** and **heightened imagination**. It's not really like sleep, because the subject is alert the whole time. It is most often compared to **daydreaming**, or the feeling of "losing yourself" in a book or movie. You are fully conscious, but you tune out most of the stimuli around you. You focus intently on the subject at hand, to the near exclusion of any other thought.".* – **Tom Harris**

If you have ever driven to work and not remembered the journey you have experienced a state a hypnosis or utilising your subconscious mind. The subconscious mind is so powerful that it is responsible for orchestrating each breath that you take, and every heartbeat. Our conscious mind is like the narrator that protects us from perceived danger and can be somewhat critical.

In hypnosis the subconscious mind which holds every experience you have had is now open for suggestions. Every time we have an experience it is stored in the subconscious. Repeated thoughts and actions build pathways in the brain which the subconscious can then form as a belief or a habit and carry out the task without conscious control. Examples of this include riding a bike, smoking, nail biting, driving or repetitive work.

However, it does not judge on positive or negative patterns of behaviour so whatever you repeatedly tell yourself will be imprinted. Examples include I am shy, nervous not good enough, clumsy, always eating, fat, thin, amazing, confident, scared of spiders, a smoker, and on and on.

Therefore, by repeatedly surrounding yourself with positive affirmations and positive reinforcement through hypnosis, *it is possible* to change patterns of behavior. This new behaviour typically takes 21 days of practice to be embedded. Which trust me is not difficult and is in fact a pleasure to do.

I became interested in hypnosis through teaching hypnobirthing. I used the techniques for both of my births and fell in love with using hypnosis for relaxation and reducing stress. I then went further and became qualified as a Hypnotherapist. At the very least hypnosis helps me to relax and reduce negative thought patterns.

The below scripts are for use in self-hypnosis. You can have someone else read the scripts for you or record them on your phone and listen to them on head phones. I have found hypnosis to be pivotal in dealing with issues around confidence and self-belief.

In addition, I find hypnosis especially useful when trying to rest after a night shift. I would find it difficult to relax after driving home and wanting to eat an entire chocolate bar and whatever I could find in the fridge!

I had the same routine after each night shift, food, shower, dark room and then I would put on a chosen hypnosis track with headphones on and be completely relaxed within a few minutes. This also had the benefit of relaxing enough for subliminal messages to really take an effect. I have used this time to build confidence, increase memory and release limiting thoughts. The thing I find so amazing about hypnosis is that it takes zero effort apart from closing your eyes and putting on earphones. I'm a fan of sleep masks to block out light too.

Sometimes I would listen to one of my own recordings and other times I would listen to sleep hypnosis through Amazon Prime (lots of different tracks that are free with Amazon Prime).

However, recording your own is very simple. You can record most scripts in MP4 format through your phones voice recorder. If you find listening to your own voice a little strange you could get a friend (whose voice you like!) to record it for you. I have included a simple script that I have written for you. This script is designed so that you can insert your own positive messages to your subconscious. The following exercise will enable you to think about what you would like to improve through positive affirmations which you can change over time. I am also happy to record scripts if you email me.

As with all types of therapy it is important that you seek medical advice for any mental health problems or epilepsy when accessing complementary therapies. Remember not to listen to hypnosis if you are driving or operating machinery (or delivering a baby or looking after patients!)

<u>Hypnosis – activity</u>

Write down three things you would like to change e.g. *Be more confident, conquer fear of heights, stop smoking*

_____

_____

_____

_____

_____

_____

_____

Write down three positive words to describe yourself e.g. *courageous, caring, funny*

_____

_____

_____

_____

_____

_____

_____

Create an affirmation (positive statement) for each of the above. e.g.

I now approach situations with confidence, I am happy to enjoy the view from the top of a mountain

I feel so happy to be able to breath easily and have fresh breath, I am proud to be courageous

My caring nature is what people love about me. Laughing and having fun makes me feel good.

_____

_____

_____

_____

_____

_____

_____

Hypnosis Script

The below script includes an introduction which will assist in gradual relaxation and a deeper to further assist with deep relaxation . There is then a section called suggestions which you can adapt to your own needs. I have included an example to get you started. At the end of the hypnosis it is important to count out and an example is included.

Close your eyes don't force them shut don't hold them shut, just allow them to gently close... take a deep breath ... hold it for three seconds ..... and as you exhale allow your body to relax ... with each and every breath that you take, allow yourself to relax deeper and deeper ...You are now going to relax each part of your body from the top of your head all the way down to the tips of your toes.

Let's begin with the top of your head, relax all the muscles around your forehead, your eyes, your cheeks and even your nose ....let go completely and relax ... just get rid of all the tension ... now move on down to your mouth, your chin and your jaw ... and just let them relax ... ... now move down to all the muscles in your neck area the front parts and the back parts … and let go …

moving down your shoulders and your upper arms and now let

them go completely …the let them droop down heavy and relaxed

… moving down to your elbows, down through to your forearms,

your wrists, all the way down to your fingertips, releasing and

relaxing … and just let go, allowing them to be totally relaxed.

And as you continue to breathe at your own pace … move down

to the muscles in your chest area … and let go now and continue

to relax … moving down to your stomach … allow all of the stress

and tension to leave your body completely … move down to the

areas around your hips, your bottom, and even your thighs … and

just let go, allowing yourself to relax more and more … move

down to the muscles in your calves, ankles, your feet and toes

… … and as you let go, allow everything in your body to relax

completely … from the top of your head, to the tips of your toes,

relax completely and deeply.

Now that you are sitting back comfortably in your chair, I want you

to imagine that it is a beautiful autumn day. The outside

temperature is just right, not too warm, and not too cold. You are

now sitting outside the garden watching the trees move softly in the warm breeze.   You recognise thee strong oak trees, and a

weeping willow that are near where you are sitting. Many of the

leaves on the trees have now changed to spectacular autumn

colours. You see the spectrum of deep reds, oranges and yellows

as they fall softly to the ground ....you hear the sound of birds

singing softly and smell the fresh autumn air, . . As you watch

each leave fall softly to the ground you marvel at their beauty as

the sun catches them and feel calm and relaxed going deeper and

deeper with each and every leave that falls,

You notice that the oak tree standing proudly in front of you has

lost most of its leaves. You notice that only 20 leaves remain on

the tree. As the wind starts to blow the leaves begin to separate

from the branches and make their way softly to the ground.... As

you watch each leaf fall to the ground, you feel yourself going

deeper into relaxation, now there are only 19, 18 leaves left...you

are going deeper and deeper. 17, 16, 15 leaves remaining on the

tree and you continue to go deeper and deeper and more relaxed

with each and every leaf that falls softly from the tree deeper and

deeper. 14, 13, 12, 11 leaves are now remaining. You feel

yourself going deeper and deeper into relaxation you feel so calm

and relaxed. Your body feels lighter and is filled with a sense of comfort and joy permeating to every cell of your body. The wind is picking up and the leaves continue to fall to the ground. 10, 9, 8, 7, 6 leaves are remaining now. And you go deeper and deeper still… more relaxed more comfortable than you have ever been before. As the last leaves fall, 5, 4, 3, 2, and one you are now in a deeply relaxed state and feel more relaxed than you have ever felt before.

Suggestions

At this point you can add any suggestions that you would like to include. Hypnosis works well with the power of three so repeating the statement three times embeds it further. I have included a few examples here for you to choose from, but you can adapt it. Make sure you keep it in the positive so as your subconscious takes the message as a statement, for example instead of:

I don't want to smoke anymore

Change it to,

I am now happy to have fresh breath and clear lungs

You believe in yourself … you are confident .. You have great qualities that others are attracted to.

At this point you can use the good qualities that you came up with in the earlier exercise.

All these qualities to grow and see yourself as others see you. You are confident kind, strong minded and believe in yourself.

You feel each day that your belief in yourself is growing. You are more confident, calm and in control in all aspects of your life now. You allow yourself to relax and give balance to your life. You care for yourself as much as you care for others. You are a role model to others and people within your care see your professionalism and confidence and feel calm and relaxed. You give hope to others and your positive outlook transfers to others. You find that each and every day you are more confident in your skills and happy to wake up each morning. You are an inspiration to others and love inspiring the next generation. You mind feels bright and open to new opportunities as your confidence and self-belief grows. You have many aspects to your life and your renewed confidence is contagious and assists you to enjoy every area of your life, your family, your work, your free time. You feel energised and empowered. You are amazing just as you are.

You have an inner peace that allows you to take control over all aspects of your life.

You are now in control and able to relax and take control of anxiety, tension and nervous energy and just simply relax and let go. You look at each situation for its positives and ways you can improve. You are now in control .. you are confident and believe in yourself.

Each time you go into hypnosis you will deepen your relaxation and relax quicker than the time before. I am now going to count from 5 to 1 and when I reach 1 you will open your eyes feeling calm and refreshed as if you have had a relaxing night's sleep. 5 beginning to feel the energy coming back to your body 4 …3….2…. and when you're ready 1 open your eyes.

3 NEURO LINGUISTIC PROGRAMMING (NLP)

"You are born with only two fears: fear of falling and fear of loud noise. All the rest is learned. And it's a lot of work!" ~ Richard Bandler

NLP or Neuro linguistic programming was first introduced by **John Grinder, a linguistic professor, and Richard Bandler, a mathematician**, at the University of California at Santa Cruz (UCSC). NLP was made more popular by Tony Robinson , one of the most acclaimed self-help Gurus of the 20th century. Tony famously said that he could help most people rid themselves of negative habits in 30 minutes.

NLP involves a practice like hypnosis, but it is not necessary to enter a hypnotic state. NLP involves removing negative imagery or events through revisiting them and then rewriting them as a script, or DVD shown in your mind.

The practice involves speeding up the negative image, rewinding it, taking out colour and basically removing the negative thought pattern or belief by destroying the script or footage.

Role modelling is another concept which involves emulating someone who has the attributes you would like to have including posture, actions, speech and communication methods. This is can be useful if your struggling to feel confident after a time of stressful event either at home or work.

"Be the person you wish to become - today. Talk like them, walk like them, breathe like them! Be them NOW!" ~ Tony Robbins

Getting into postures commonly associated with power can convince your brain that you are powerful. Such a posture is the power pose where you put your hand behind your head and lean backwards on a chair for extra effect you can put your feet on the desk although this is sometimes not practical!

"People wait for something to happen in order to be happy; the key is to be happy regardless." ~ Richard Bandler

For NLP a script is not necessary, however below is an exercise that you can adapt yourself to go through a past experience or thought pattern that may now be impacting your behaviour, such as a fear of public speaking, needle phobia, fear of spiders. It is important that you imagine that you are watching the event passively as if you're watching a movie as a protection against the event. If you decide to look at a photo album you can imagine you are placing Perspex above the image. If it's a tv screen you are passively watching as if you are an actor in the movie so therefore detached from the event.

NLP exercise

Think of an event or fear that you would like to get rid of

_____

_____

_____

_____

_____

_____

_____

Decide if you would like to view the event as a movie or imagining looking through a photo album. You can record the instructions of what to expect if this makes it easier.

_____

_____

_____

_____

_____

_____

_____

_____

When you have decided on a fear or event to rid yourself of you can now find a comfortable position and close your eyes. Imagine the scene as if you ae looking through a photo album or watching it on the screen. Watch it in real time first.

Next watch the footage again but this time speed it up so that the characters in the movie look comical , imagine music playing in the background similar to circus music if this makes it more ridiculous.

Keep running the footage back and forth back and forth over and over again. The aim is to make the memory no longer effect you. You can make the image black and white then fuzzy until it disappears completely

Another aspect is to imagine you are then destroying the movie reel or DVD with a hammer or burning the image if it is a photo.

Next think of a positive image of what you would like to achieve.

This could be making a presentation or getting your dream job.

Make some notes here of what you want to achieve.

Once you have that positive imagine bring it up big and walk into

the image or movie that you have created. Imagine yourself as the

main character and see and feel what the experience would be

like. Next capture this feeling in an image of you achieving your

goal and take it with you back into the present. This image we are

going to keep and will form a anchor for when you want to achieve

your goal.

Although this method is simple, it is very powerful so worth the time to develop and use. I have used this method for women fearful of birth, either through a belief of a negative birth or remembering an experience. They create a new movie where the experience is what they would like to achieve. They then recreate this image or movie over and over again to make it a default for when they go into labour.

4 GRATITUDE

"One of the most tragic things I know about human nature is that all of us tend to put off living. We are all dreaming of some magical rose garden over the horizon instead of enjoying the roses that are blooming outside our windows today." ~ Dale Carnegie

Research has found that keeping a gratitude diary makes people feel happier and more grateful for things they may have stopped noticing in their lives.

In addition, Gratitude is a positive thought and our brains cannot think a positive and negative thought at the same time.

The more that you start to look for things that you are grateful for the more you will begin to see how fortunate you are. You then get used to looking for the positive instead of looking for the negative.

The next section and activity are to use different methods to start bringing gratitude into all areas of your life.

This is a very simple activity that can have a huge impact. I also get my children to do this but instead of asking them to write it down I ask them what the best part of their day was. They enjoy doing this most of the time!

My favorite responses have been "the lift "after a full day at Alton Towers and on another occasion "spending time with my family". It has made me realise that we all take a lot of pleasure in the simple things like a picnic in the park or a bike ride instead of activities that require expensive days out.

The below activity is to get you used to compiling a gratitude list. I would recommend starting with writing 5 things that you are grateful for each day. Surprisingly this can be difficult at first, people think they must look for large events to write down instead of finding the positive in everyday events.

Gratitude list

Write down below five things each day that you are grateful for. Continue to note them down over the next few days. I would then recommend using a specific notebook for this as it will fill up quickly. Get one that makes you feel happy. I use a cheap notebook with a unicorn on the front! I have listed five examples below to give you a started.

1. I am happy and grateful to be in a warm home.

2. I feel blessed to get cuddles from my children in the morning.

3. I am grateful for my friends supporting me and making me laugh.

4. I'm happy to get a parking space at work without any effort!

5. I am happy to have had time for a coffee and magazine before picking the children up.

<u>Your Gratitude List</u>

Day one

1. _____

   _____

   _____

   _____

   _____

2. _____

   _____

   _____

3. _____

_____

_____

_____

_____

4. _____

_____

_____

_____

_____

5. _____

_____

_____

_____

_____

Day two

1. _____

_____

_____

_____

_____

2. _____

_____

_____

_____

_____

3. _____

_____

_____

_____

_____

4. _____

_____

_____

_____

_____

5. _____

_____

_____

_____

_____

Day three

1. _____

_____

_____

_____

_____

2. _____

_____

_____

_____

_____

3. _____

_____

_____

_____

_____

4. _____

_____

_____

_____

_____

5. _____

_____

_____

_____

_____

5 GOAL SETTING

Within midwifery and nursing refection forms part of our practice. Reflection is now utilised in revalidation to assist in looking at situations that have happened and putting a plan in place to improve them. If you have identified something that you would like to change one method is to set goals.

This can be achieved by simply writing them down, however, to fully embed the goals you can activate different parts of your brain through visualisation.

People worry that they may not be able to visualise, but everyone is fully capable of visualisation. Think of your front door. Whereabouts is the letterbox? You can probably bring up a picture of what it looks like.

Sports professionals use visualisation to practice for a race, game or event in their minds first. Scientists have found that the same muscles and brain activity are activated when visualising than when they do it for real. It's almost like having a trail run.

However, we are still able to improve on this, your sense of smell and hearing can be used to amplify the effects. Using as many senses as possible when visualising helps to create stronger neural connections.

If you think of someone walking through the grass several times, eventually a path will form. This is the same with brain waves and neural connections, the more you repeat something the stronger these connections will be.

In addition using your sense of smell and sound increases your ability to call up the visulisation. If you think about a time when you are feeling low, if you put on music that links to a happy time it can uplift you, this may be a song you have heard on holiday, the first dance song from your wedding , or even a song from your favorite movie. You can almost be taken straight to the memory.

This is because audio imprints on the brain as part of the memory. Another strong sense, is the sense of smell. Have you ever smelt sun cream and it has reminded you of a holiday? How about freshly cut grass, Are you getting a memory of a happy summer? We remember sounds and smell as part of our memories.

You can use this to your advantage when using visualisation to embed it further in your mind.

Goal setting – Activity

"Where focus goes, energy flows. And where energy flows, whatever you're focusing on grows. In other words, your life is controlled by what you focus on. That's why you need to focus on where you want to go, not on what you fear. When you next find yourself in a state of uncertainty, resist your fear. Shift your focus toward where you want to go and your actions will take you in that direction." ~ Tony Robbins

Find a quiet place and write down 5 goals which you would like to achieve. Don't edit the goals by what you think is possible. Write down exactly what it is you would like to achieve. Some possible examples may be

Lose weight

Gain more confidence

Graduate from master's course

Learn a new skill

Learn how to drive

Change your current role.

_____

_____

_____

_____

_____

_____

_____

_____

_____

_____

_____

_____

_____

_____

Next make the goals more specific to what you want to achieve

and set a date. For example. I want to be 10lbs lighter in 3 months.

_____

_____

_____

_____

_____

_____

_____

_____

_____

_____

_____

_____

_____

_____

Now you're ready to get your other senses involved. Write down how you will feel once you are 10lbs lighter. Imagine the smell of the gym as you work out looking fit and healthy. Think of what music you may be listening to at this new lighter weight. Look

down at your body what does it look like now you are fit and

healthy. Imagine which outfits you can now wear, look into a

mirror in your mind and visualize how it looks. Do this for each of

the five goals.

_____

_____

_____

_____

_____

_____

_____

_____

_____

_____

_____

_____

_____

_____

Your final goal explanation may look something like this.

1. I am going to lose 10lbs in 3 months by 25th March. I attend the gym five times a week and enjoy the smell of chlorine and lemongrass as I enter the gym. My clothes fit well on my now healthy frame. I look in the mirror and see how great I look in my outfit. I enjoy listening to my playlist as I work out on the stepper. My favourite song to work out to is eye of the tiger. I enjoy being so healthy and feeling so good.

You can see that the goal is now quite specific and easy to identify when it will be completed. Look at your list each day. I find looking at a different goal each week helps to really embed it. I read the goal then close my eyes and really imagine what it will feel like with every sense. Once you have reached the goal you can replace it with another. You may want to write your completed goal down into a Goal Achieved book which allows you to see your accomplishments.

Individuals also enjoy making a visualisation board with pictures of their goals that they can look at each day. It's an enjoyable activity where you can search online or in magazines for images of your

goals. This can then be placed in an area that you will see it often.

6 TIME MANAGEMENT

Don't let the fear of the time it will take to accomplish something stand in the way of your doing it. The time will pass anyway; we might just as well put that passing time to the best possible use."

— Earl Nightingale

Within the health industry it is difficult to manage your work life balance. This can be because your service is overstretched, or you are covering more than your normal work load. Midwives and nurses will often stay later to assist co-workers or care for patients. However, this can then have an impact on your family and social time.

Time management suggests we have control over time which we don't. However, we can prioritise how we spend our time. I know the suggestions I am about to make may not sound achievable, but they can work.

However, you need to first journal how long you spend time on different activities. It can be quite a shock when you first do this. You may find you spend a lot of time watching TV checking social media, sleeping, travelling!

"You can't have a plan for your day, 'til you have a plan for your life." ~ Tony Robbins

Activity

Choose two separate days to write down exactly how you spend your day. Include *everything* you do and how long each activity takes. It may look something like this.

06:30 Alarm goes off. Snooze button. Asleep 10 minutes.

06:40 Alarm goes off again. Check social media and emails 20 minutes.

07:00 Downstairs to shower. 15 minutes.

07:15 Kettle on put breakfast out for kids. Wake children up. Youngest wants a cuddle 15 minutes.

07:30 Downstairs for breakfast and get uniforms ready. Children wanting to watch TV, wanting something different for breakfast. New breakfast made. School menu checked. Not liking anything on menu. Packed lunch made. All still in PJs .

07:50 Rush to get ready, dress children, husband to take children to school.

08:00 Leave house for work.

And continue through the day including driving times, meetings , lunch (I know it sounds like a luxury on a busy shift) and what happens when you return home.

When I did the same activity, I noticed that although I felt I was running around all day there were times when I could have used my time more wisely.

 For instance, I was struggling to fit in any exercise as I needed to get the children ready for school, get to work and then was so tired by the end of the day that all I wanted to do was go home, relax and see my family. I was also staying up most nights until about 11:30. This mean that when my alarm went off in the morning, I felt like I needed an extra hour. Also, sometimes I would start a boxset and instead of watching one or two I'd watch the lot and stay up even later.

Use the space below to record 2 separate days of activity;

"Time is the most valuable coin in your life. You and you alone will determine how that coin will be spent. Be careful that you do not

*let other people spend it for you." — **Carl Sandburg***

Monday

06:00-07:00

_____

_____

_____

_____

_____

08:00-09:00

_____

_____

_____

_____

_____

10:00-11:00

_____

_____

_____

_____

_____

12:00-13:00

_____

_____

_____

_____

_____

14:00- 15:00

_____

_____

_____

_____

16:00 – 17:00

_____

_____

_____

_____

18:00 -19:00

20:00 – 21:00

22:00 -23:00

00:00 onwards

_____

_____

_____

_____

_____

Saturday

06:00-07:00

_____

_____

_____

_____

_____

08:00-09:00

_____

_____

_____

_____

_____

10:00-11:00

_____

_____

_____

_____

_____

12:00-13:00

_____

_____

_____

_____

_____

14:00- 15:00

_____

_____

_____

_____

16:00 – 17:00

_____

_____

_____

_____

18:00 -19:00

_____

_____

_____

_____

20:00 – 21:00

_____

_____

_____

_____

22:00 -23:00

_____

_____

_____

_____

_____

00:00 onwards

_____

_____

_____

_____

_____

"An hour of planning can save you 10 hours of doing." ~ Dale Carnegie

In order to decide what to spend my time more effectively on I then followed the following activity.

1. List areas of your life where you would like more time.

_____

_____

_____

_____

_____

2. Devise a plan of change. This included walking up early to exercise at 6 a.m., going to bed earlier, and restricting TV at night.

_____

_____

_____

_____

_____

3. It doesn't mean getting rid of things that you enjoy, it just means finding the times of day when you are most productive. You can then use that time for **must** do tasks.

4. If you have time slotted in for something you enjoy such as watching TV or playing video games or even searching social media set time aside at your least productive time and set a time limit.

5. Put your phone out of reach at night as it is very tempting to check your phone before you go to bed and when you

wake up in the morning. This can affect you sleep cycles at night due to the type of light emitted from your device.

6. Use an alarm that is not on your phone. If you are turning off the alarm you will be tempted to check your emails or social media. This can result in an extra hour that you could have used to get yourself ready at a relaxed pace. It can also bring unwanted negativity into your space when you wake up.

These measures at the very least will help you to identify how you are already spending your time. Have you ever noticed that sometimes when you do less you can feel more tired? Designing your day to include exercise and time with your family can give you more energy and feel more productive.

7 CONCLUSION

I hope this journal has given you some tools that you can use to improve your mental and physical wellbeing. Health and wellbeing departments within your workplace may have services that you can access for free , such as meditation classes, coaching and reduced-price complementary therapies.

In addition, if you work in the NHS you can also get discounts on gym memberships, holidays and days out. Although it sounds counterproductive you do have to spend time on yourself to enable you to care for yourself.

The below quote is from an autobiography of a nurse between 1900-1925. The identification that caring and nurturing yourself has an impact on the care you give to others is as relevant today. I sincerely hope that staff in healthcare settings are given the resources and time to care for themselves .

Four impressionable years spent in a number of very different hospitals convinced me once for all that nursing, if it is to be done efficiently, requires, more than any other occupation, abundant leisure in colorful surroundings, sufficient money to spend on amusements, agreeable food to re-establish the energy expended, and the removal of anxiety about illness and old age;

yet of all skilled professions, it is still the least vitalised by these

advantages, still the most oppressed by unnecessary worries,

cruelties, hardships and regulations."

— ***Vera Brittain, Testament of Youth***

ABOUT THE AUTHOR

Michelle Mckay is a midwife, wife, ,mother and educator. She is interested in hypnotherapy for helping with positive childbirth and helping people cope with fears, phobias and low self-esteem. Her interest in hypnotherapy has led to becoming qualified as a hypnotherapist. She enjoys working with all age groups to bring positivity and release their inner strength and ambitions.

Made in the USA
Coppell, TX
12 November 2020